POSITIVE PRACTICE

5 Steps to Help Your Child Develop a Love of Music

Christine E. Goodner

© 2018 Christine E. Goodner

Positive Practice: 5 Steps to Help Your Child Develop a Love of Music
First Edition, July 2018
Brookside Suzuki Strings, LLC
Hillsboro, Oregon

Editing: Lucie Winborne
Publishing & Design Services: Melinda Martin, MartinPublishingServices.com

Positive Practice: 5 Steps to Help Your Child Develop a Love of Music is under copyright protection. No part of this book may be used or reproduced in any manner whatsoever without written permission except in the case of brief quotations embodied in critical articles and reviews. Printed in the United States of America. All rights reserved.

ISBN: 978-0-9991192-3-5 (print), 978-0-9991192-4-2 (epub)

DEDICATION

To all the parents
who work with their children
as they learn to play an instrument.

May you know
you're making a difference,
even if your child
never tells you themselves.

INTRODUCTION
POSITIVE PRACTICE:
5 STEPS TO HELP YOUR CHILD DEVELOP A LOVE OF MUSIC

WHAT IS POSITIVE PRACTICE?

Does positive practice mean everyone is happy and positive for every minute of our practice time together?

Is it even realistic to expect practice to be positive?

In Benjamin Hardy's new book *Willpower Doesn't Work: Discover the Hidden Keys to Success*, he talks about current research on happiness, and how it gives people the false idea that we must *feel* positive for positive results to be happening.[1]

As parents, when we practice music with our children, we find out quickly that there is a range of emotions, both our own and our children's, in the span of a week, and even one practice session. Does that mean we're doing something wrong? Is it a sign that music is not our child's "thing"?

When I talk about positive practice, I am not implying that everyone will feel "happy" all of the time. It's a good goal, and it's wonderful when that happens.

But practicing an instrument and taking music lessons are hard work. Even professional musicians struggle with practice and many say while they love playing their instrument, they don't always love practice. So, even for the pros, practice is not always happiness and positivity.

I hear from many parents that when their child is just starting lessons, they want to see if their child likes it, or they just want their child to have fun. I think that is a great approach to a painting class, or trying out soccer.

I would argue, though, that learning an instrument needs to be seen as a long-term commitment. It's a skill that needs to be developed over time, like language acquisition or learning to read.

INTRODUCTION

As parents, we understand the value of literacy. For those who love reading, we want to see that love develop in our children as well. That doesn't mean, though, that every step along the way, as our child learns to read, is fun. It doesn't mean there aren't challenges. We keep at it because we know it's part of the process, and because the end result is worth the hard work to get there.

Learning an instrument is very similar. It's difficult and the beginning stages take a lot of effort and support from the parent. But that doesn't mean it has to be a negative experience either.

When we practice with our children, we can address different parts of practice and tailor how we work with our child to their individual needs. We can think of being on the same team, working together through assignments for the next lesson.

After teaching students for the last nineteen years, and raising two daughters whom I practiced with, I have seen the importance of helping a child develop their own internal motivation and a love of music through practice.

Practice feels positive when we are making progress. It feels positive when we establish a good working relationship with our child and they are willing to do the hard work of practice.

Practice is positive when we don't see the child's role as obeying our demands, but rather a chance to coach them as they learn to focus and stick with something even when it's not easy right away.

This guide will take you through the process I use to help parents learn to practice more positively.

It doesn't mean practice won't be hard or frustrating at times. Your child may not want to get started some days and won't magically feel like practicing before you ask them to. Even professional musicians have these struggles.

However, we *can* help make practice more positive and help our child practice in a more engaged way. It gives us a roadmap to make things easier and more productive.

INTRODUCTION

When I recently asked over one hundred parents what the best part of practicing with their child was, they answered: seeing their child's ability to play the instrument improve, the bond that developed between them and their child, and seeing their child develop character qualities such as focus, perseverance, and a work ethic.

Those are the positive results we like seeing as parents and this guide will help you learn to do just that.

A NOTE TO PARENTS

Thank you for investing in your child's music education. There are so many benefits children gain by studying music that go way beyond the actual skills they learn on their instruments.

Adults who studied music while growing up often report benefits such as learning to focus, appreciation for music, and the ability to break down big problems into little, manageable pieces.

Practice at home isn't always easy for the students or the parents trying to help their child practice. I often hear from parents that home practice has become a daily fight with their child. That is not a sustainable situation for learning music or for our relationship with our children.

It is the job of the music student to practice. However, as parents we can have a profound impact on the environment they practice in, their understanding of what practice entails, and helping them develop practice skills.

We can't control our children's moods or their behavior but we can help them learn to do so. We can help them learn to transition into practice successfully and we can practice with them (or help them practice) in a way that builds momentum and motivation. We can also learn to focus on and reward good behavior and practice skills we see developing so over time these things improve.

INTRODUCTION

This guide will lead you through a five-step process to help you, the parent, reduce conflict with your child as they learn to practice their instrument.

This process is based on my own experience, research, and work with families over the last nineteen years. It has been my privilege to provide parents with solutions, because I know the impact practice has on families and on students' long-term success in music and life.

INSTRUCTIONS
HOW TO USE THIS GUIDE

I recommend reading this guide all the way through to get an idea of what is involved in this process.

Then I would take one section at a time and take a close look at practice with your child at home with that section in mind. In each section there is a question to ask yourself. These five questions will become part of your daily practice routine, and will help you create peaceful, productive practice sessions.

A series of questions after each chapter will guide you in thinking through and applying the ideas to your situation.

There are pages available for taking your own notes and answering questions in this guide. If you purchased a digital copy, or would rather print separate pages out to write on, you can download a copy of the journal pages at PositiveMusicPractice.com.

This is where actual change will happen: answering the questions and then testing the ideas with your child.

Not every idea will work for your family, but many can be modified as needed. I am happy to help you problem-solve if you join the online workshop group that goes with this guide.

Transforming your home practices into peaceful and productive times with your child is possible, and I am excited to help you do just that.

THE PARENT'S ROLE

DEVELOPING THE MINDSET FOR PEACEFUL, PRODUCTIVE PRACTICE

Your child has started lessons and you are part of the process: either by practicing with them closely or at least by making sure they have time for daily practice.

Your role as the parent is more important than you may realize.

Research shows that one of the biggest factors in a music student's long-term success is their parents' commitment to the process.[2]

I think that's because, as parents, we treat activities differently if our children are just trying them vs. committed to them long term. For example, my kids went through phases where they hated brushing their teeth–it was like a form of torture to get them to do it.

But because we wanted them to have healthy teeth as adults, we couldn't just decide this activity "wasn't for them" and let them stop. Instead, we found ways to make it more tolerable and enjoyable until it eventually became a habit.

We got colorful toothbrushes and bought tubes of toothpaste that had cartoons on them, and sang children's songs about brushing teeth until eventually they brushed their teeth without a fight.

When I give parent talks at workshops and other events, I like to start off by asking parents why they want their children to study music or what benefits they know about from studying music long term.

THE PARENT'S ROLE

We come up with great lists, including:

- Focus
- Love of music
- Perseverance
- Attention to detail
- Empathy
- Developing a work ethic
- Learning how to learn

As parents we may not be overly concerned with whether our child keeps playing their instrument into adulthood. However, most of us want them to develop characteristics on the list of benefits I just mentioned.

If we want to develop these things, and we decide learning music is a value in our family, then we need to find ways to help them stick with it until it becomes a habit of their own, like I did with my kids and their tooth brushing.

Does practice in your house right now mean frustration and arguments?

Please know it doesn't have to be that way. This guide will take you through the same steps I used to practice with my own children and to help parents I work with in my studio practice more peacefully and productively with their children.

I encourage you to start by committing to helping your child learn to practice, which is its own skill, in addition to learning the skills to play an instrument.

Please keep an open mind as we go through these lessons. Practice that works for your child may look really different than you imagine it should. I encourage you to remain open and creative. You may be surprised by what works for your family and child.

While sometimes this feels like extra work to us adults, it is good to remember that a one-size-fits-all approach rarely works for anything in life.

If our children are going to grow up to be successful at anything they do, they will need to learn to work with their own unique set of strengths, and to work around, and build up, the areas that are harder for them.

We are using music to learn these skills.

THE PARENT'S ROLE

QUESTIONS TO ANSWER

What is the hardest part of starting practice in your house?

What would you like to see change?

THE PARENT'S ROLE

What is the hardest part of starting practice in your house?

_____

_____

_____

_____

_____

What would you like to see change?

_____

_____

_____

_____

_____

BEFORE WE START

A LITTLE DISCLAIMER

I can't promise you'll never have conflict over practice again. What I can say is that if you put these ideas and concepts into practice, you will be doing what you can to help your child practice with less resistance.

As an adult who loves playing the violin, I don't always feel like doing the actual practicing. I hear the same from many professional colleagues. What most of us love is performing, making music with other people, and the feeling of having improved because we practiced.

You don't need to convince your child practice isn't hard, isn't sometimes frustrating, or that they should cheerfully love every minute. Instead, we're teaching them how to overcome resistance to something that is challenging. That, I can say as a parent of college-age children, is a life skill worth building.

When we want the results, how do we get there?

I hope you'll take the ideas in this guide to heart, put some serious thought into the questions at the end of each section, and these ideas will help you in a very practical way. Some of the concepts might help right away and others will help over time.

Either way, I hope they make starting daily practice at your house much more pleasant!

POSITIVE PRACTICE

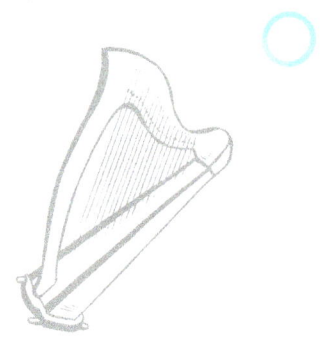

5 Questions Every Parent Should Ask to Keep Home Practice Positive & Productive

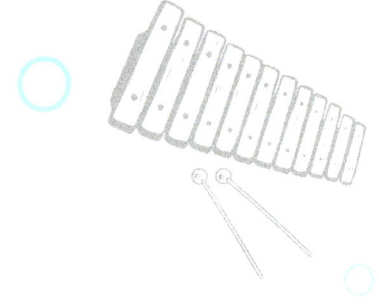

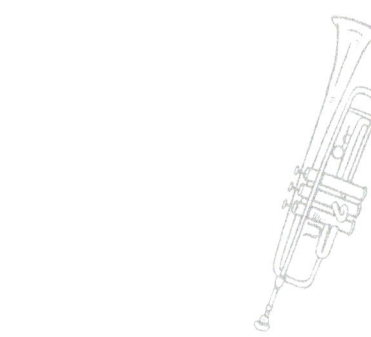

POSITIVE PRACTICE 1

PLANNING

DID YOU START TODAY'S PRACTICE WITH A CLEAR PRACTICE PLAN IN MIND?

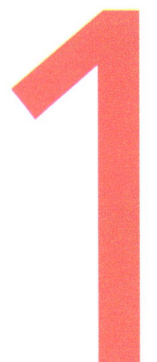 # PLANNING

DID YOU START TODAY'S PRACTICE WITH A CLEAR PLAN IN MIND?

HAVE A PLAN

It is tempting to think that planning for practice is an unnecessary step, we don't have time, or we'll just make it up as we go and get the same results. This couldn't be further from the truth.

Being intentional about how we run practice sessions sets our child up for success. You only need to spend a minute or two preparing.

Complete the following sentences:

Today I will be: _____ .

This is your chance to make a goal for yourself. Today I will be patient, or totally present, or only positive in my comments. We can all work on something.

In today's practice our main goal is: _____ .

Usually there is one major skill a student is working to improve: getting a beautiful sound, holding the instrument, focus . . . . There are many possibilities. If you are not sure what this should be, please ask your teacher.

Three things we should accomplish today are: _____ .

You may have a whole list of things to practice. What are the top three for today? Anything else you get to is a bonus. Set priorities before you start.

PLANNING

A WORD ABOUT CREATING A MUSICAL ENVIRONMENT

If we set out to become fluent in a second language, we have to do more than take a class and memorize new vocabulary.

The best way to become fluent is to have lots of conversations in that language and to immerse yourself in a culture where there is no option but to learn the language and start to communicate in it.

I am quite sure I would never become fluent in Japanese, for example, if I never heard the language being spoken around me, or if I only heard it once in a while. A huge part of your child staying motivated and excited about music is creating a musical environment at home.

Listening to music that our children are learning is really important to their musical development. So is listening to music by performing artists on their instrument, especially.

What is the point of learning an instrument?

To make music!

If we aren't developing a love of listening to music, a big piece is missing. Students who develop an interest in a certain style of music, performer, or composer have an extra dose of motivation to draw from.

Often students want to learn an instrument because they saw a performance or heard music that they wanted to play someday. If this type of experience is what sparked their interest, it will likely also be what keeps their interest going as well.

PLANNING

POSITIVE PRACTICE 2

ATTITUDE

WERE YOU ABLE TO GET PRACTICE STARTED WITHOUT A BATTLE OF WILLS WITH YOUR CHILD?

2 ATTITUDE
WERE YOU ABLE TO GET PRACTICE STARTED WITHOUT A BATTLE OF WILLS WITH YOUR CHILD?

HOW YOU START MATTERS

We live in an instant-response culture. We expect things to start when we push a button. We like microwaves and instant everything.

Sometimes when we decide it's time to move from one activity to the next, we want our children to react and get on board right away. We might even give ourselves a warning that it's almost time to start practicing, but forget to tell our child.

What I've learned as a parent and teacher is that how we transition into and start practice makes all the difference.

How you start really matters.

Some children have a much more difficult time than others leaving one activity to start a new one. One principle I always talk to parents about is working with our children's stage of development and unique needs.

If it always seems your child should move more quickly into practice, they may need a little more transition time.

It is especially hard to relate to this issue if we parents can move quickly and easily from one task to another. Please know it's normal for it to take time to do this. We can reduce conflict if we just allow time for this process.

What can you do to help your child come into the practice room ready to practice? I have a few suggestions.

ATTITUDE

1. Create a Schedule or Routine

This is key. If your child knows practice always happens after snack time, they'll start to mentally prepare in advance out of habit. Sometimes we have to vary practice times depending on the day of the week and other activities. That's fine, too. At the very least, come up with a routine for each day to help your child transition.

2. Give Advance Warning

We may think to ourselves, "Oh, it's almost time to practice," but if we don't share that information with our child, we may really take them by surprise.

If I'm in the middle of the chapter of a good book, or a good conversation, I too would feel out of sorts having my instrument put into my hands to practice.

Even if your child seems to be doing nothing, they may be deep in thought and need the transition time. A five-minute warning is a smart idea. Some parents use a timer, which takes away any debate about whether it has really been five minutes or not.

3. Give Choices

"We can practice now or after dinner."

"We can practice before or after a snack."

Giving your child an option, other than just yes or no, can be a great way for them to build ownership over their practice. If you have an older child I would encourage them to write down three goals for their practice that day. This can be done on a small whiteboard or in a notebook.

Transitioning to practice might involve organizing their thoughts and getting ready to focus on goals they help create. Of course, all this has to be done while keeping the assignments from their teacher in mind.

ATTITUDE

4. Start with a Game or Transition Activity

Starting out the practice session with something fun and engaging is a great way to draw your child into the process.

What appeals to each child is different but here are some ideas:

- Buy a deck of note-reading flash cards and see how many your child can get correct in one minute.
- With a young child, start with a fine motor activity such as picking up a small object with each finger and thumb in turn.
- Get a stress ball (one for each hand is even better) and practice a round, squeezing motion. This is good for finger dexterity and flexibility and is very relaxing.
- Work on reading rhythmic patterns (you may have assigned materials or you can find some great ideas through MusicMindGames.com).

The possibilities are endless!

MORE THOUGHTS ON GETTING STARTED

What is your child like when they transition to and from other activities such as school, homework, bedtime etc.? Thinking through how you help them transition to and from these activities can help you with strategies specific to your child.

In my Suzuki Early Childhood training we learned the importance of the practice environment. For children whose parents are involved in practice, YOU, the parent, are the practice environment.

We're not just talking about the décor in the room or limiting distractions but the emotional environment. Are we setting it up to be calm and productive?

We can't control whether our children feel grumpy about practice. And we have no control over things such as whether they've gotten enough sleep or had a bad day. However, we can make an impact through the way we approach practice sessions.

ATTITUDE

QUESTIONS TO ANSWER

> Do you have an ongoing practice routine?

> Do you have a system for warning your child when it's almost time to start practice?

> What ideas from this lesson could you implement in your practice times this week?

> How well does your child transition to other activities?

ATTITUDE

Do you have an ongoing practice routine?

_____

_____

Do you have a system for warning your child when it's almost time to start practice?

_____

_____

What ideas from this lesson could you implement in your practice times this week?

_____

_____

How well does your child transition to other activities?

_____

_____

POSITIVE PRACTICE 3

ATTENTION

WHICH PART OF TODAY'S PRACTICE HELD YOUR CHILD'S ATTENTION THE MOST?

3 ATTENTION

WHICH PART OF TODAY'S PRACTICE HELD YOUR CHILD'S ATTENTION THE MOST?

HOW WE PRACTICE

We've already discussed a bit about how we, parents, are the practice environment for our child(ren). We help set the emotional environment or feel of practice.

If daily practice feels like a fight, none of us are going to look forward to it the following day. If practice (or at least some small part of it) feels like we spent quality time together and maybe even had some fun in the process, then it's a more appealing activity to repeat.

Here are some principles that help shape a good practice session:

First, if you are working with a very young child, especially as a beginner, the best way to make practice work is to break it into a few small, shorter sessions. The key is to stop before your child is "done" or asks to stop.

Keep it short, upbeat, and leave them wanting more. Over time you'll stretch out the length of practice. For now, build a feeling that practice is pleasant, short, and enjoyable!

On the opposite end of the spectrum, if your child is a teenager I recommend they set the length of time they will practice and a goal of what to accomplish with their teacher.

Don't be surprised if you have to remind them to get started. My own parents had to remind me all through high school, and I'm so glad they didn't give up on doing so.

My biggest tip here is: only make positive comments or ask questions. Let the teacher give corrective feedback. Also, don't hesitate to contact your teacher if you feel they need to know something about the quality of practice going on at home.

In my book *Beyond the Music Lesson*[3], I interviewed Suzuki teacher-trainer Ann Montzka-Smelser, who shared a great insight on this topic. She said that Olympic athletes are cited

ATTENTION

as saying the most important words their parents said to them were "I love to watch you play!"

"I love to see how hard you're working."

"I love hearing you play."

"I love to see the progress you're making."

This is what your child most needs to hear from you.

Take it from a mom who has parented two teens–even if they seem to dismiss your comments, or roll their eyes at you when you say these things, they are taking them to heart. This is the best thing you can do to support them in the process of practicing when they have otherwise taken over all the management of what and how to practice.

While you are still actively practicing with your child, it's important to keep in mind what motivates them.

Is it games?

Is it boxes to check off or a list to follow?

Is it upcoming performances?

Is it teaching a skill to someone else?

We learn this by close observation and by trial and error along the way.

This can be particularly hard if your child is really different from you in how they learn and are motivated. Maybe they love games but you find them tiring. Or you want to incorporate games but they would just rather get on with playing their music.

ATTENTION

Spending the time to find out what motivates your child to learn new things is so worth the time and effort.

This is also a great opportunity to get to know your child in a way many parents don't. What you learn can be applied to helping them learn to work on other school subjects and meet many other goals in life. It is very powerful knowledge to have.

For more insight into this topic I highly recommend reading Michele Horner's book, *Life Lens: Seeing our Children in Color*.[4] My co-host Abigail Peterson and I had the opportunity to interview her on the *Beyond the Music Lesson* podcast (Season One, Episode 6). Horner gives specific practice ideas for parents and teachers that are tailored to the way a child learns best.

A note about Feedback

I recently had over 100 parents who practice with their children participate in a survey about what it's really like to practice together. One thing that many parents brought up was how difficult it is to give feedback to their children in a way their child will receive well.

In my own experience this was the hardest part of working together effectively. It is easy for the delivery of feedback to cause conflict between parents and their child during practice.

Sometimes I let my own frustration and lack of patience show. Others times I tried to point out something to work on very carefully. And sometimes I felt like I was giving a compliment and even that caused conflict.

WHAT IS A PARENT TO DO?

I don't have a magic answer for everyone, although I sure wish I did. Every child responds so differently, and depending on their maturity and stage of development this changes over time.

ATTENTION

Basic principles I like parents to keep in mind when giving feedback:

Say what we want to see more of

Children will do more of whatever we focus on. I recommend helping your child notice even tiny bits of progress as they happen. Your child likely notices the mistakes, and if they tend to get frustrated and feel like it's "hard," pointing out any bit of progress we see helps everyone involved feel like all the hard work is worth it.

As parents, we may have to train ourselves to think of what is positive first. It is a skill I have developed as a teacher in order to work more effectively with students, and I recommend parents work to develop it too.

Talk about *what*, not *who*

Here is another tip I can pass on that I have learned from teaching: if I talk about *what* needs to happen (the wrist needs to stay relaxed) instead of *who* needs to do it (you need to relax your wrist), there is usually a totally different response.

We can give feedback more effectively if we address practice tasks this way. It is easy to get an emotional response if our child feels like we are saying they are doing something wrong, even though that is not our intention. It just takes a moment to rephrase what we notice needs to happen, and it is a really effective way to make feedback more positive.

Notice how your child responds to different types of feedback

Of course, everyone is a bit different. What does not faze one child at all, as far as feedback goes, may result in another child melting down in tears. It may make no logical sense to us, as their parents, at all.

Whether or not it seems like a reasonable response, these types of reactions by our children give us information about how they best receive feedback.

ATTENTION

Focus on working *with* your child to get the result you want

In lessons, I like to ask parents and their children to agree on how they can help each other remember particular practice spots. For example, sometimes we'll come up with a nonverbal signal everyone agrees to. Even if your teacher doesn't address this you can have the conversation with your child at home, at the start of the week.

"How can we remember to work on this together?"

"What can I do to remind you of this while you're playing?"

Questions like these allow for conversation about what will help and can help you, the parent, get on the same team with your child as you work to make the assignment easier over the week of practice.

Along these same lines, another important principle for working with students just learning to practice is to ask a lot of questions. I think it's very important to remember that:

Practice shouldn't mean "an adult tells me what to do."

Even with the most compliant of children you will eventually get pushback from this type of approach. Not only that, but if we ever want our children to practice independently and effectively, they have to learn to be a part of the thought process that makes practice work.

We can ask questions like:

- "What does your teacher want you to work on in this piece?"
- "How did that sound?"
- "How can you improve this section?"
- "Did it get better?"
- "Is that what you wanted?"

ATTENTION

This sort of conversation is not wasting practice time, even though it can feel that way sometimes to parents. It's actually building ownership and teaching children to think deeply about what they are playing and what they want to improve.

This helps practice and playing their instrument become something they are deeply invested in, rather than something we are making them do.

QUESTIONS TO ANSWER

> Can you see any changes that you need to make after reading this section?

> How can you change practice to foster motivation, ownership, & interest?

ATTENTION

Can you see any changes that you need to make after reading this section?

_____

_____

_____

_____

How can you change practice to foster motivation, ownership, & interest?

_____

_____

_____

_____

POSITIVE PRACTICE

TIMING

DID THE PRACTICE END BEFORE YOUR CHILD ASKED FOR IT TO END?

4 TIMING
DID THE PRACTICE END BEFORE YOUR CHILD ASKED FOR IT TO END?

END WITH THE BEGINNING IN MIND

So far we've talked about how to start practice and how to work with our child while practicing.

I would argue that how we end practice is one of the most important parts of this process.

The most important thing you can do to help create motivation and reduce conflict when it's time to practice is to end each session with something fun and enjoyable. That is the feeling that is going to stick in your child's mind between today's practice and when it's time to start again tomorrow.

Even professional musicians I've spoken with have talked about how making time to play something they love on a daily basis is a critical part of their practice.

LET'S TALK ABOUT WHAT THAT MIGHT LOOK LIKE

Note: You know your child best, and you'll get to know them better through the process of working together. I suggest you try some of the ideas I'm going to talk about, but also be creative and try your own.

What makes your child leave the practice room with a huge smile on their face?

What do they think is just plain fun about learning, and playing, their instrument?

# TIMING

This is what we want to find out. This is the carrot dangling in front of them during the rest of practice and the thing that makes them (over time) get excited about getting started.

It's okay not to love every part of practice. Often when we let students know that is the case by saying something like, "You don't have to love this part but, you do need to know how to do it," they are much more accepting of working on it.

It is important to balance this out, though, by including parts of practice that are just plain fun.

As a teacher, I know that students need to practice scales, work on tone production, and practice good technique. But I'm also under no illusion this is what excites them about music or makes them love to play their instrument.

Suggestions for Achieving Balance During Practice

Let your child pick the last thing they practice.

"What piece should we end on today?" is a great question to ask. There is no wrong answer here. Remember, we are building momentum for tomorrow.

Allow time for improvisation & free play.

This is really motivating to many of my students. If they are old enough to be left to their own devices, leave the room and let them play for the fun of it. If they are younger and need your supervision with the instrument, then let them experiment without input, unless a safety issue is involved.

If your child tends to get off track because this is all they want to do, often just promising them the time at the end will help the assigned part of practice move along well.

TIMING

Learn something by ear, or sight-reading time.

Let your child pick something fun to either figure out by ear or to sight-read, with your teacher's blessing. This should be something that is not part of the regular practice assignments from your teacher, or an upcoming piece you will work on with your teacher in the future.

For example, I have had students figure out the Happy Birthday song by ear for a family member, or the theme song from a favorite movie. There is all sorts of sheet music online and in your local music store that your child could play just for the fun of it. See what is exciting and motivating for your child.

Repeat a piece from earlier in the practice that your child especially enjoyed.

It's always good to end on a high note and this is a simple way to do that. I use this technique often in lessons and highly recommend it.

Have your child teach you something on their instrument.

Some students are really motivated by teaching a skill to someone else. They get really excited about showing you something they know, but you don't. This can be a great way to help students feel confident about their skills.

However you choose to end practice, the idea is to end with something that both makes your child feel successful and that they enjoy.

Think of it as the dessert. It may take a week or more of doing this consistently before you see a change, so don't give up if it doesn't happen right away.

TIMING

QUESTIONS TO ANSWER

> How have you been ending practices before now?

> Does practice end on a positive note most days?

> What ideas could you implement from this lesson to change the dynamic or make the end of each practice session more positive?

TIMING

How have you been ending practices before now?

_____

_____

_____

Does practice end on a positive note most days?

_____

_____

_____

What ideas could you implement from this lesson to change the dynamic or make the end of each practice session more positive?

_____

_____

_____

POSITIVE PRACTICE 5

RESULTS

WHAT WAS THE END RESULT OF TODAY'S PRACTICE?

5 RESULTS

WHAT WAS THE END RESULT OF TODAY'S PRACTICE?

- A piece of music got easier to play
- A technical skill was improved
- A clearer, more beautiful sound was produced
- Your child played with more expression or artistry
- Your child was able to focus and concentrate (even if for a short time) while playing

ASSESSMENT

At the end of each practice session take a quick assessment of what was accomplished. We want our practice sessions to be both peaceful and productive.

If practice is conflict free and your child is enjoying the process, that is a great start. The next step is to be sure we are also improving our skills. This last question will help you keep this in mind. As practice starts to get easier in your home, it will be easier to focus on the results we get from our practice sessions.

Being involved in practice with our children can be an intense experience.

All the parents I know and work with want their child to do well, to work hard, and to be successful.

Sometimes how we go about arriving at that goal looks far different for our children than it would have for us when we were young, or than we pictured it looking when we thought about starting lessons.

If there is one thing I've learned about parenting, it's that we can have a huge impact on our kids if we help them navigate their own particular challenges and strengths, rather

RESULTS

than fit them into some kind of mold shaped from all the things we should, must, and must do.

As parents we need to think beyond getting practice done efficiently and quickly. Instead we need to think about what helps our child get started, what approach works best while they practice, and how we end practice so they are more interested in coming back to it again tomorrow. We can't control our child's behavior in practice and we're not responsible for doing the work for them, but we set the tone for the practice environment.

Do our children feel understood?

Do they feel respected?

Are we helping them develop a love of music?

Are we providing an opportunity for fun with the instrument at the end of each day, or at least most days?

Are they in an environment where they are hearing music or seeing live performances often?

RESULTS

As a parent and teacher, I know that while these ideas are simple, they are not always easy.

I know many of you are thinking, "If you only knew my child!" Or maybe you wish you'd had this information years ago before bad practice habits were formed. But I want to let you know it's not too late. Even professionals are always changing and improving how they practice, and so can you and your family.

A big reason I started writing about this topic is because that was me. I struggled to practice with my kids when they were small, and I struggled to do it all "right." Sometimes I didn't realize what my daughters actually needed to make it work for them.

As I said at the beginning of this guide: I can't promise there won't be any more conflict, but I can say that what I have shared has worked over and over again with families I teach.

Not every child will keep playing music into adulthood, but I do hope our children love and appreciate music into their adulthood. I hope we'll all understand each other better because we worked so closely together and I hope they'll know how much I love to see them play.

Whatever your and your child's specific music goals are, I hope you can put these ideas into practice. You have a special opportunity to work closely with your child through music. I hope you will be able to start practice with less conflict and have more peaceful and productive practices after using the ideas in this guide.

Wishing you all the best!

RESULTS

PRACTICE ASSESSMENTS

POSITIVE PRACTICE: 5 STEPS TO HELP YOUR CHILD DEVELOP A LOVE OF MUSIC

The next three pages contain assessment sheets that can be used for parents, teachers, and independent practicers as a way to gauge how practice is improving over time.

You can find PDFs of these worksheets to download at www.positivemusicpractice.com.

How to use the parent assessment: go through this checklist to check in and take a careful look at how practice is improving.

I recommend doing so daily until practice becomes more positive and productive on a regular basis. At that point, go through the questions at least every couple of months. Each student's practice approach and needs will change over time, however these questions still apply. If you start to notice practice is becoming more frustrating and less positive, it's time to look at these questions on a regular basis again.

How to use the teacher assessment: give parents of students you work with a copy of the assessment to fill out and return back to you. I recommend going over the answers together. You can use it as a part of parent-teacher conferences or talk about it at the start of a lesson, but helping parents find solutions should be the main goal.

Having families fill out this assessment should help you gain insight into what practice is really like for them at home and can help you see where further support is needed. It can be a great conversation starter that will benefit teacher, parent and student alike.

Independent practice assessment sheet: I have also included an assessment for students who are practicing independently to fill out. This can be shared with the teacher to help start the conversation about more effective independent practice.

ASSESSMENT

PRACTICE ASSESSMENT FOR PARENTS

1. Did you start today's practice with a clear practice plan in mind?

   ☐ Yes   ☐ No   ☐ Sometimes

2. Were you able to get practice started without a battle of wills with your child?

   ☐ Yes   ☐ No   ☐ Sometimes

3. Which part of today's practice held your child's attention the most?

   _____

4. Did you end the practice session before your child asks for it to end?

   ☐ Yes   ☐ No   ☐ Sometimes

5. Did one of the following happen as a result of today's practice? Star each item you'd like more help with. (Circle or check all that apply)

   - a piece of music gets easier to play
   - a technical skill is improved
   - a clearer, more beautiful sound is produced
   - your child plays with more artistry or expression
   - your child is able to focus (even briefly)

ASSESSMENT

PRACTICE ASSESSMENT FOR TEACHERS

1. Did you start each day's practice with a clear practice plan in mind?

    ☐ Yes   ☐ No   ☐ Sometimes

2. Are you able to get practice started without a battle of wills with your child?

    ☐ Yes   ☐ No   ☐ Sometimes

3. Which part of practice holds your child's attention the most?

    _____

4. Do you end practice sessions before your child asks for it to end?

    ☐ Yes   ☐ No   ☐ Sometimes

5. Does one of the following happen at each day's practice? Star each item you'd like more help with. (Circle or check all that apply)

    - a piece of music gets easier to play
    - a technical skill is improved
    - a clearer, more beautiful sound is produced
    - your child plays with more artistry or expression
    - your child is able to focus (even briefly)

ASSESSMENT

PRACTICE ASSESSMENT FOR INDEPENDENT PRACTICERS

1. Did you start today's practice with a clear practice plan in mind?

    ☐ Yes   ☐ No   ☐ Sometimes

2. Were you able to get practice started without procrastinating or arguing with your parents?

    ☐ Yes   ☐ No   ☐ Sometimes

3. Which part of today's practice held your attention the most?
    _____

4. Did you have a clear idea for when practice should end?

    ☐ Yes   ☐ No   ☐ Sometimes

5. Did one of the following happen because of today's practice? Star each item you'd like more help with. (Circle or check all that apply)

    - a piece of music got easier to play
    - a technical skill improved
    - a clearer, more beautiful sound was produced
    - you played with more artistry or expression
    - your ability to focus increased

RECOMMENDED RESOURCES

BOOKS

Beyond the Music Lesson: Habits of Successful Suzuki Students by Christine E. Goodner

Helping Parents Practice by Edmund Sprunger

Life Lens: Seeing Our Children in Color by Michele Horner

PODCAST

Beyond the Music Lesson on Apple Podcasts and Overcast

WEBSITES

http://www.SuzukiTriangle.com

http://www.ChiliDogStrings.com

http://www.PluckyViolinTeacher.com

ACKNOWLEDGMENTS

There are so many people who helped make this project a reality. I want to give a big thank you to everyone who gave feedback about the wording, concepts, and ideas in this guide.

Specifically, thank you to **JEFF GOINS** and **DEANNA WELSH**: two of my mentors who were an integral part of helping me make this project a reality.

Thank you to my editor **LUCIE WINBORNE** for all your encouragement and your excellent work. You are a delight to work with.

Thank you to my cover designer and formatter **MELINDA MARTIN**. As always, you do an amazing job making my projects look professional and beautiful. I was so glad to work with you again.

Thank you to the following friends and colleagues who gave feedback along the way including: **NEIL FONG GILFILLAN**, **VALENE GOLDENBERG**, **CHRISTY PAXTON**, **ABIGAIL PETERSON**, **ANGEL FALU GARCIA**, **JENNIFER YARBROUGH**, **SWAN KIEZEBRINK**, and **NAMRATA SHARMA**.

Thank you to the **SUZUKI TRIANGLE COMMUNITY** for being a wonderful to place to share ideas.

As always, a big thank you to my husband **MIKE** who is endlessly supportive and my biggest fan.

Christine E. Goodner

ABOUT THE AUTHOR

CHRISTINE GOODNER is a violin & viola teacher, author, podcaster, and speaker in Hillsboro, OR. She started playing the violin at the age of three and raised two daughters who studied music throughout high school.

Christine is passionate about helping parents find better ways to practice with their children & support them in their music studies. She is also the author of the Suzuki-licensed book *Beyond the Music Lesson: Habits of Successful Suzuki Families* and has been published in the *American Suzuki Journal*.

Christine frequently blogs, podcasts, and gives talks and workshops on topics related to music. You can connect with her and her latest work at ChristineGoodner.com.

CONNECT WITH THE AUTHOR

WEBSITE
http://ChristineGoodner.com

EMAIL
Christine@SuzukiTriangle.com

FACEBOOK
https://www.facebook.com/ChristineEGoodner

DOWNLOAD EXTRA JOURNAL PAGES
https://www.PositiveMusicPractice.com

SOURCES

1 Benjamin Hardy, *Willpower Doesn't Work: Discover the Hidden Keys to Success* (Hatchette Books: New York, New York, 2018).

2 Daniel Coyle, *The Talent Code: Greatness Isn't Born. It's Grown. Here's How* (Bantam Books: New York, New York, 2009).

3 Christine Goodner, *Beyond the Music Lesson: Habits of Successful Suzuki Families* (Brookside Suzuki Strings, LLC: Hillsboro, OR, 2017).

4 Michele Monahan Horner, *Life Lens: Seeing Our Children in Color* (MCP Books: Minneapolis, Minnesota, 2016).

www.ingramcontent.com/pod-product-compliance
Lightning Source LLC
Chambersburg PA
CBHW061145010526
44118CB00026B/2879